ENDORSEMENTS FOR BEACONS

Roberto Escamilla is a man of deep faith
remarkable wisdom. This book is filled with tr
his experiences that you will not want to miss.

Tom Albin
*International Director of Development
and Missional Coordinator
United Christian Ashrams, Ruston, LA*

The word "sage" is a term that conjures up thoughts of wisdom, prudence and good judgment through reflection and experience. We seldom hear that word used anymore because there aren't many people who give honor to the word. But there is one who lives among us who represents the truth of the Gospel and how a life should reflect an intimate relationship with our Lord and Savior Jesus Christ! His name is Roberto Escamilla, and in this book, "Beacons of Hope," he shares his wisdom and his heart with us. Indeed, he is for me a modern day "sage" of the Gospel.

Bishop Robert E. Hayes, Jr. (Retired)
*2004-2016 Bishop of the Oklahoma Area United Methodist Church,
United Christian Ashram Board Member,
The Woodlands United Methodist Church, Bishop in Residence*

Brother Roberto Escamilla's passion for Jesus and the Kingdom of God is contagious. His pursuit of greater knowledge and fresh experiences with Jesus brings hope to his life and to his teaching. I am blessed to call him mentor, brother, and friend.

Matt Henson
*Executive Director
United Christian Ashrams International*

Roberto Escamilla's long and distinguished career of service for Christ and His Church is shared in twelve brief chapters about the Christian life. He gives us an insight both into the Gospel and into the ministry of his mentor E. Stanley Jones. This is an inspirational book!

Bishop Scott J. Jones
Texas Annual Conference, The United Methodist Church

I have been blessed with hearing and learning from Brother Roberto for decades. His lifelong impassioned plea for more grace for himself, his loved ones, his brothers and sisters in Christ, and a world hungry for Jesus, testifies to his humility and deep desire to draw ever nearer to Christ and share His saving grace with a hurting world. I am profoundly blessed to call him my brother, my teacher and my friend.

Georganne Leonard
Member of The Ashram Four

Dr. Escamilla's book not only provides excellent insights on the work of Dr. E. Stanley Jones but also offers very encouraging personal reflections based on his pastoral work, as well as questions for personal reflection. *Beacons of Hope* is exactly what our world needs today— an integral message of love expressed in words and charitable practices. May God lead us, through Dr. Escamilla's work, to reflect God's grace in everything we do.

Hugo Magallanes
Associate Dean for Academic Affairs, Director, Hispanic-Latin@ Ministries Program (MAP), Associate Professor of Christianity and Cultures at SMU- Perkins School of Theology

The next time someone asks me to explain the global influence of E. Stanley Jones and the Ashram Movement, I will recommend "Beacons of Hope" by Roberto Escamilla, the last living member of "The Four." Even more than the compassions and inspirations that accompany every page, this book is really about what Thomas Aquinas calls, *latitudo cordis*, the expansion of the heart. Read it for a heart expansion in adoration and awe.

Leonard Sweet
Best-selling author, professor (Drew University, George Fox University, Evangelical Seminary), publisher (The Salish Sea Press), and founder of preachthestory.com

Also by Roberto Escamilla:

Come to the Feast: Invitational Evangelism, 1998
Prisoners of Hope: Essays on Life's Journey, 1981
A Feast of Life, 1972

BEACONS OF HOPE

Dr. Roberto Escamilla

DEDICATION

To Anne Mathews-Younes, President of the E. Stanley Jones Foundation, in recognition of her work in the re-publication of E. Stanley Jones' books, which now offers a vital link of his ministry to future generations.

To the United Christian Ashram International (UCAI) Board, its Executive Co-Directors, Tom Albin and Matt Henson, Office Manager, Lisa Chandler, and all Ashram leaders and the entire Ashram family in the United States, Canada and around the world.

To my loving, supportive family and to our son, Paul, who even as a toddler felt the "call" into the ministry and now preaches with seldom found, powerful eloquence.

"With God all things are possible."

Matthew 19:26

CONTENTS

FOREWORD

I am delighted to write the foreword to this latest book by my dear friend and mentor, Dr. Roberto Escamilla, who has provided extraordinary leadership to the Christian Ashram movement and a lifetime of service to the mission of the church.

Roberto has been involved with the Christian Ashram for now almost sixty-five years and has faithfully served as a member of the Ashram Four, designated by E. Stanley Jones in 1971 to represent the soul of the Christian Ashram. In addition, Roberto served as the President of the North American Christian Ashram Board from 2009-2014, and continues to offer distinguished leadership to the Ashram movement and has been fully implementing the 'learnings' he received from his Ashram mentor, and friend, E. Stanley Jones.

Dr. Escamilla is well known as a Christian leader and has embraced tasks on a scale as large as global Christianity, such as inclusion and support of Hispanic clergy and as small as conversations with individuals to offer an evangelical witness for faith in Jesus Christ. Whether he was working as a denominational leader or serving as a translator who helped English-speaking preachers, including E. Stanley Jones, bring the gospel to Spanish-speaking congregations, Roberto has offered a faithful and robust witness to God's people. Roberto has a partner in his ministry, his wife Dorothy, his faithful companion on their life's pilgrimage and constant support to his ministry.

In 2013, Roberto was a recipient of Perkins School of Theology, Southern Methodist University Distinguished Alumnus Award for his effectiveness and integrity in service to the church, distinguished service in the wider community, and for the extraordinary scope of his ministry.

His passion for evangelism and gift of encouraging others in their lives and ministry has been a hallmark of Roberto's life and he has never ceased to serve wherever God places him. He often speaks of the loving and gracious hand of God leading him in service to our increasingly secular society where the Gospel must be proclaimed to address the hunger of the human heart. He knows that in every pew, there is at least one broken heart and Roberto preaches to that person with love and skill as he proclaims the grace of God who can overcome all estrangements and brokenness.

Roberto was once advised "to wait for the slow growth of seeds," and this he has done faithfully. The harvest has now come in and we rejoice in its bounty as we look on in wonder at his magnificent life and legacy and affirm Jesus is Lord!

Anne Mathews-Younes

The E. Stanley Jones Foundation

ACKNOWLEDGMENTS

My gratitude, first and foremost, to Anne Mathews-Younes and the E. Stanley Jones Foundation for suggesting I write this book.

Special thanks to my daughter, Marlene, who was baptized by E. Stanley Jones, at the Texas Ashram in Kerrville in 1957. She has edited and transcribed my handwritten notes, creating the narrative for this book.

Also, deepest thanks to my wife, Dorothy, who is always willing to help me with scriptural references and has been a constant and loving support throughout my life in ministry.

My grateful appreciation to the First United Methodist Church in Ada, Oklahoma and to the senior pastor, Brian Matthews, for providing space for me to continue my writing, as well as opportunities to volunteer in support of church ministries.

My gratitude to the Co-Executive Directors of UCAI, Tom Albin and Matt Henson, the other members of "The Four"— John Davis and Georganne Leonard, as well as all current and former officers of the UCAI Board.

My sincere appreciation to Lisa Chandler, for her immense help, in countless ways, and for keeping the "Ashram fires going" as she serves as our office manager in Ruston, Louisiana.

And lastly, my deepest admiration to my friend and mentor, the late E. Stanley Jones.

INTRODUCTION

In all honesty I never intended to write another book. Despite feeling that I was done with the rigors of writing, I nevertheless believe in divine guidance which often comes to us in unexpected ways. Therefore, when the gracious invitation of Anne Mathews-Younes arrived, offering to publish my final book, I yielded to divine guidance. I am so grateful for this opportunity.

Anne has always been a source of inspiration to me and my wife, Dorothy. She reminds me of her grandfather. Her spirit, intelligence and entrepreneurial gifts are truly from God.

The themes that I am writing about were selected from familiar topics in the Christian Ashram vocabulary. I decided to write about these specific subjects as a lasting tribute of appreciation for the multiple gifts I have received through my involvement in the Ashram movement. At the time of this writing, (September 2021), I am honored and privileged to be a member of the original "Four," the guardians of the Ashram, as named by E. Stanley Jones in 1971. The inaugural meeting of "The Four" took place February 23, 1973 on the occasion of the burial services of the ashes of Brother Stanley. The original "Four" were Bill Berg (1910-2013), Rev. Dr. Gordon C. Hunter (1924-1997), and Dr. J. T. Seamands (1916-2004) and myself.

Although E. Stanley Jones had suffered a serious stroke in 1971, and died in early 1973, he was able to attend the 1972 World Ashram Congress meeting in Jerusalem. It was at that first international Ashram meeting that he announced the appointment of the "The Four" to be "the soul of the Ashram". He hoped that the naming of "The Four" would enable his vision of the Ashram to continue.

"The Four" were not selected from a specific criterion of being more spiritual or better than the rest of the Ashram constituency. They were, however, men and women who had experienced personal transformation through the Ashram and were committed to protecting the integrity of the movement by ensuring that the basics of the Ashram principles and traditions would be maintained and used when creating new Ashrams around the world.

Karl Barth, whom I greatly admire, was once asked to describe his life. He commented, "My life is all grace!" That is how I feel, as well. I would also affirm the comment of another much-admired theologian, Paul Tillich, who said, "Another word for grace is 'in spite of'", then adding, "Accept the fact that you are accepted, despite the fact you are unacceptable."[1] Amen!

My earnest prayer is that as you, both clergy and laity, read and reflect on the content of these chapters, that you will be blessed with the seeds of contemplation and prayer that would fill your heart and mind. My sincere hope and prayer is that what I share of my own personal experience will also be a blessing for your life, and that you will bless others as you share the love of Jesus with all whom you meet and encounter throughout your days.

Jesus is Lord!

Prayerfully,

Roberto Escamilla

Fall 2021

E. Stanley Jones and Roberto Escamilla, Chile, ca.1961

1

A PERSONAL TRIBUTE TO E. STANLEY JONES: A MAN FOR ALL SEASONS

"You did not choose me, but I chose you and appointed you..."
(John 15:16, NIV)

I first met E. Stanley Jones at a Christian Ashram in Kerrville, Texas, in the summer of 1956. I was deeply impressed by his demeanor and his knowledge of the Bible *and* his skill in preaching to the wide and diverse audience. When we returned to the Ashram the following year, he graciously baptized our baby daughter, Marlene. She now serves as a member of the board of UCAI.

As the years went by, E. Stanley Jones and I became better acquainted and he subsequently invited me to be his travel companion and interpreter for Ashrams in Mexico, Puerto Rico and several South American countries. It was indeed a great honor and privilege to work with him in this new capacity.

I'll always be indebted for the rich legacy of Jones' mantle of influence over my life and ministry:

- He helped me to understand evangelism and that the Gospel message applies to body, mind and spirit.

- He taught me how to preach for a response, with an authentic appeal, which often included extending an invitation to the altar.

- He helped me expand the impact of my personal counseling by illustrating that asking questions and really listening to persons in their brokenness can have a transforming impact.

- He taught me much as I learned how to do my ministry more effectively, but especially to *love every person I encountered with an unconditional love*. This practice has made all the difference in the world.

So, I will be indebted to him for the rest of my life. What I am doing now is to channel my energy to further the work that he started through the Christian Ashram. My goal is to continue to reach people and preach the Gospel and share the love of God with all persons.

Questions for Personal Reflection

We are submitting the following questions for personal reflection and small group discussions. Please use the rest of the pages for personal journaling or notes.

1. Even though you may not have known E. Stanley Jones in person, you have surely read some of his books. What quotes or ideas have been especially meaningful to you and why?

2. How do you understand the idea of loving every person with unconditional love?

3. How do you explain Brother Stanley's vitality?

JESUS: WHAT'S IN A NAME?

"She will give birth to a son, and you are to give him the name Jesus, because he will save his people from their sins." (Matthew 1:21)

As Jesus came among men, he did not try to prove the existence of God, he brought him. He lived in God, and men looking upon his face could not find it within themselves to doubt God.[1]

I love the hymn, "Jesus, Jesus, Jesus, there's just something about that name!"[2] And then every time we pray, we conclude the prayer with, "In Jesus' name, Amen!" Well then, does using the name Jesus make any difference? Yes, it makes all the difference in the world! Its use affirms a foundational belief in the power and love of Jesus. E. Stanley Jones repeatedly stated the following: "You cannot understand the Kingdom of God unless you first understand Jesus, and you cannot understand the Holy Spirit until you first *say* Jesus, and you cannot understand life until you first understand Jesus." The name of Jesus is powerful and knowing Jesus is to know love.

Jesus is another name for grace. "Out of his fullness we have all received grace upon grace." (John 1:16) Every moment of our lives we experience grace, even in the ordinary moments of daily existence. We can't earn grace. We can only receive it as a gift. "For it is by grace you have been saved, through faith—and this is not from yourselves, it is the gift of God." (Ephesians 2:8)

E. Stanley Jones wrote a book entitled, *The Word Became Flesh*. In this powerful book, he gives expression to the divinity of Jesus, the Son of God, who came to redeem the world. God tried many other ways to reveal himself, with Noah, David, John the Baptist, and finally, through Jesus, as the supreme revelation of God.

Theologians write about the Jesus of history and the Christ of faith, the cosmic Christ. We affirm that Jesus is God's highest revelation of himself. Jesus is God incarnate. During the Advent Christmas season, we rejoice about the miracle of the incarnation, the Word became flesh. (John 1:14)

The Ashram embraces this miracle of the incarnation and in the Ashram tradition, we affirm that "Jesus is Lord."

Questions for Personal Reflection

We are submitting the following questions for personal reflection and small group discussions. Please use the rest of the pages for personal journaling or notes.

1. Jesus, there is something about that name. What in your personal experience is "something" about His name?

2. How have you experienced grace in your life, lately and today?

3. What does it mean for you to that "the Word become Flesh?

3

LIFE: WHAT'S IT ALL ABOUT?

"I have come that they may have life and have it in all its fullness." (John 10:10 NEB)

How many times do we find ourselves asking, "What is life really all about?" We ask that question in times of joy, as well as in times of sorrow. We are often speechless at the mystery of it all.

The well-known Christian author, Adam Hamilton, Senior Pastor of the Church of the Resurrection, comments that when he is asked to speak to an organization, he always asks, "What shall I speak about?" Most respond, "You can talk about anything you wish, as long as it is *inspirational.*" That's an excellent answer. I agree that when people hear a sermon, they usually hope to glean something useful and inspirational from it. As a pastor, I always pray that people will be sufficiently inspired to face their personal challenges, whether illness, disabling conditions, racism, fear, or any of the other relentless difficulties life presents us with.

E. Stanley Jones has much to say about LIFE and in particular the life of Jesus Christ *and* our lives lived in Christ!

The life of Jesus was a truly human life. Jesus met life as a man. He called on no power for his own moral battle that is not at your disposal and mine. His character was an achievement. Everything he laid before men in the works spoken in the Sermon on the Mount had gone through his own soul. They were livable, for he was living them.[1]

As we face life, Jesus is inescapable, for he is the epitome of that upward urge for life. You ask me to define life, I cannot. But I have seen life. There it stands, Christ: I fall in love with life and living as I see him.[2]

And finally,

You and I have one great thing to invest, and that is our lives.

We may invest our lives in money, or buildings, or pleasure, but if we do, what happens? The only bank that will not break is the bank of human character. If we invest in people, then our investment is deathless![3]

So "What is life really all about?" It is about living our lives with Christ-like love. That is the very best way to face life, and in so doing, the mystery of life dissolves in the face of love.

Questions for Personal Reflection

We are submitting the following questions for personal reflection and small group discussions. Please use the rest of the pages for personal journaling or notes.

1. Have you ever found yourself asking the question, "What is life all about?" What answers did you get? Silently think about it or share aloud your reflections.

2. Is your life an abundant life? Explain?

3. Is your hope a gift? If so, how?

4. How many times have you laughed today? Brother Stanley used to say, "If you find nothing to laugh about, go look in your mirror." For further information about laughter, I would certainly recommend a chapter on laughter in Len Sweet's great book, "The Jesus Prescription for a Healthy Life." (Abingdon Press, 1996).

5. What are your thoughts about aging? Brother Stanley would say, "No one is old. We are just getting older."

4

PREACHING: THE POWER
OF THE WORD

*"How could they invoke one in whom they had no faith? And
how could they have faith in one they had never heard of? And
how hear without someone to spread the news? And how could
anyone spread the news without a commission to do so?
(Romans 10:14)*

One of the most meaningful aspects of ministry is preaching. The technical term for preaching is homiletics. I try to ensure that my sermons are culturally informed, evangelical, intellectually respectful, hermeneutically correct, and emotionally charged.

I always ask God before I preach to deliver me from falling into the pit of "platitudes." I define platitudes as the tendency to use certain phrases or "clichés" that congregations have heard so many times that they have become meaningless, like a coin worn as smooth as a river rock by constant usage. So, my prayer is, "Lord, deliver me from preaching platitudes," and of course, this means we preachers must find new ways of telling the "old, old story of Jesus and His love in new, fresh ways."[1] So, just how do pastors do this? We need to:

- Be mindful of the local culture.

- Consider using contemporary verses of the Scripture, such as Eugene Peterson's translation, *The Message.*" E. Stanley Jones always used the Moffat translation of the Bible, which during his time was the most contemporary version available.

- Consider consulting the original languages (Greek and Hebrew) to understand the original intent of the biblical passage as this will help your parishioners understand the context of your words.

- Preach with a sensitivity and empathy for the brokenness and the hurts of persons in the congregation, using what Fred Craddock identifies as the "exegesis" or context of the congregation.[2]

- Keep in mind what John Wesley meant by preaching as harvesting a "passion for souls."

- Be conscious of what the message means to you *personally and testify to that personal meaning.*

- Preach for a "response", whether explicit or implicit.

- Be aware that "briefer is always better." A sermon should not last longer than 15-17 minutes. Leave the congregation wanting more from you.

- Don't use illustrations borrowed from a book. The pastor before you may have already used it, particularly if you are preaching from the Lectionary format.

- Don't look at your notes if you can avoid them. Connect with people by looking into the eyes of your congregation's members.

- Don't hesitate to use emotion whenever appropriate.

- Preach about virtually anything life offers, good or bad, so you can lead the congregation to be inspired to face life unafraid!

If you are a layperson, please don't be overly critical of your pastor. (Imagine what it feels like to walk in his/her moccasins). Pray for your pastor before he or she preaches and while he or she is preaching.

I've never used much humor when I preach. It may be because I feel that people do not come to worship to be entertained. They come to worship God and to be inspired. I believe that the idea of starting every sermon with a joke or a funny story is unnecessary and if my attempts at humor fall flat, it could ruin my message. I do believe though, that God has a sense of humor and so does Jesus.

I've often felt that a great deal of preaching fails because it lacks sufficient emotion, the congregation just hears words and does not experience the feelings behind the words. Somehow, we must find a way to touch the hearts and minds of the congregation in order to give rise to a response. I do not mean that we should seek excessive emotion. There is a difference between *emotional preaching* and *preaching with emotion*. I'm talking about the latter and that can make all the difference in terms of the impact of your message!

Questions for Personal Reflection

We are submitting the following questions for personal reflection and small group discussions. Please use the rest of the pages for personal journaling or notes.

1. Are the sermons you hear meaningful in your personal life?

2. Do you ever find yourself praying for your preacher?

3. What type of sermon would be helpful in your life? How?

5

HOPE SPRINGS ETERNAL: KEEP THE FLICKERING FLAME BURNING IN YOUR HEART

"May the God of hope fill you with all joy and peace as you trust in him, so that you may overflow with hope by the power of the Holy Spirit." (Romans 15:13)

One of the most familiar quotes is from Alexander Pope, "Hope springs *eternal* in the human heart." It is so true! I have lived it and believe it with all my heart.

I have been known to use the phrases, "A hope that refuses to die," or, "A never-dying hope." When I've been asked to sign my book, *Prisoners of Hope*, I usually write "Let the flickering flame of hope keep burning in your heart forever." It is a good message for those of us who are fortunate enough to be "prisoners" or captives of Christ's hope and wish to share with others. There are days when the flame of hope may be faint, especially when "the storms of life are raging," but it is still very present, and we can draw on even that flickering hope to sustain us.[1]

Some of us experience despair, the opposite of hope. Even the Apostle Paul refers to his experience of despair. "We are hard-pressed on every side, but not crushed; perplexed, but not in despair." (2 Corinthians 4:8) Paul is telling us that in spite of our distress and despair, we do not give up or give in because we have eternal hope.

You and I can have hope despite all that life throws at us. We can learn ways to counter despair and learn how to cope. Imagine the significant difference unyielding hope would have in our work, our relationships, our faith, our present, and our future.

According to E. Stanley Jones, Christians are not exempt from the pains, sorrows and sicknesses that come upon all of us, but they are given an inner set of the spirit, by which they rise above these calamities, by accessing the very fury of the calamities themselves. Jones reminds us that when a storm strikes an eagle, he sets his wings in such a way that the wind currents send him above the storm by their very fury. The set of the wings does it. We can also set our souls to rise above the fury and ride the current of the Holy Spirit which provides us hope and supports us.[2]

How can we survive without hope? We cannot! Hope is absolutely essential. But we must have a proper understanding of hope. It is not wishful thinking. It is not thinking that things will get better on their own. Rather, hope is based upon our belief in a God of hope. "May the God of hope fill you with all joy and peace as you trust in him, so that you may overflow with hope by the power of the Holy Spirit." (Romans 15:13) A God of hope leads us through the darkest valley to a mountaintop.

Questions for Personal Reflection

We are submitting the following questions for personal reflection and small group discussions. Please use the rest of the pages for personal journaling or notes.

1. What is your personal definition of hope?

2. Are there times in your life when you have felt as if you've lost all hope? What did you do about it?

3. Hope is so much more than wishful thinking. If so, what is genuine, authentic hope? How does it work?

4. Are you happy, purely happy? Can you appropriate the meaning of pure joy? It is interesting to note that the word joy appears fifty-seven (57) times in the New Testament. It is obviously important. How do you experience joy?

6

CONVERSION: THE WONDER OF A NEW BEGINNING

"... How can someone be born when they are old?" Nicodemus asked. "Surely they cannot enter a second time into their mother's womb to be born!" (John 3:4)

Whatever definition for conversion we may have, and there are many, for the purposes of the Christian Ashram experience, we would affirm that conversion is a joyful "returning to God."

Sometimes this 'returning to God,' may happen in a highly emotional way and other times in a quiet manner, like the soft blowing of the wind.

Conversion, to be real and lasting, must include both a *vertical* and a *horizontal* dimension. The vertical dimension has to do with our relationship with God in heaven, and the horizontal dimension has to do with our relationships with our neighbors, family and friends.

In the Christian Ashram tradition, there is always one night when the evangelist preaches about conversion and at the conclusion of the sermon, extends an invitation for persons to come forward (also known as the altar call) and experience conversion, this return to God. The conversion moment may be for the first time or be a renewal of an earlier conversion decision and experience. There is undeniably power in preaching about conversion, for conversion transforms lives.

We know that the Gospel is relevant for today. However, we need to interpret and communicate the essential meaning of conversion in the context of our secular, pluralistic twenty-first century. As we are challenged to welcome the dawn of a new millennium with courage and vision we must formulate new ways to tell the old, old story of Jesus and His love.

E. Stanley Jones' book, *Conversion*, describes his own conversion this way,

Everything I wanted occurred, reconciliation with God, with

myself, with my brothers and sisters, with nature, with life itself. I was reconciled. The estrangement was gone. The universe opened its arms and took me in. I felt as though I wanted to put my arms around the world and share this with everyone.[1]

In Jones' continued effort to put his arms around the world, he very frequently preached on 'conversion' and noted that at least two-thirds of a typical church congregation members are *not* converted. However, he found that people are hungry to hear the Gospel and very often only need to be asked to come forward and return to God.

We do not have many revivals these days, occasions where the invitation to conversion is offered, and there seem to be fewer and fewer full-time evangelists who are leading revivals. In an earlier day, revivals were a very powerful experience for many of us.

What then must happen in order to keep alive this fundamental experience of conversion? What I believe is needed is a clearer understanding of conversion, and its tangible benefits and impact. With conversion, the individual becomes sensitive to a range of universal concerns, such as social justice, climate change, and world peace.

A word now about God's magnificent creation— It does matter.

We must protect God's creation and honor it. "Do not come any closer," God said. "Take off your sandals, for the place where you are standing is holy ground." (Exodus 3:5.)

There is a possibility that the traditional language used in the old-fashioned "revival" meetings no longer communicates the power of conversion to the younger generation, especially the millennials.

However, regardless, the issue remains: Persons need to be converted *today*, just as they did for centuries. But how? Let me point to some specific ways to cultivate a climate in a local church, where conversion may take place. Some of these suggestions are for the pastor and many of them can be offered by laypersons.

- Consider preaching about the power of conversion. If the meaning of the word conversion is confusing, you may want to use words such as transformation, or a return to God.

- Create a climate where conversion is not only talked about and accepted, but encouraged.

- Have a well-planned and executed program to welcome visitors and have a fellowship time before and after every service.

- Follow up with visitors by sending a personalized card or letter, signed by the pastor and/or lay person.

- Add the visitor's name and address to your newsletter mailing or e-mail list. You may wish to invite them to your church and can use Facebook, Instagram and Twitter social media platforms to engage visitors.

- Contact visitors before the following Sunday and encourage them to join worship again.

- Encourage your pastor to preach about conversion (or a related subject) at least 2 or 3 times a year, and extend an invitation for conversion or re-dedication to a Christian life.

- Plan to hold a one day evangelistic service (revival) each year with a powerful guest evangelist/preacher.

- Offer follow-up classes or the opportunity to join a church membership class.

- Offer a Prayer Group that meets weekly and include prospective converts and new members in the prayers of the group.

- Set yearly conversion goals.

- Offer a course about the importance of evangelism, to broaden the knowledge of your congregation.

There are many Biblical stories of deep conversions that provide us with great insight and motivation to keep alive and illustrate the meaning of conversion, or to use the traditional terminology, being born again.

Therefore, I would suggest illustrating one of more of these well-known conversions in your preaching:

- The woman of Samaria (John 4:4-26)

- Nicodemus (John 3:1-17)

- Zacchaeus (Luke 19:1-10)

These illustrations provide excellent sermon material and resources for study groups. For further study, please read the book *Conversion* by E. Stanley Jones.

In summary, conversion is a miracle of God's grace. We cannot explain it or produce it, but we must be open to God's invitation to return to Him.

Questions for Personal Reflection

We are submitting the following questions for personal reflection and small group discussions. Please use the rest of the pages for personal journaling or notes.

1. Do you feel that you are truly converted? Did it happen suddenly, or has it been a gradual process?

2. Have you ever tried to help someone else toward conversion? How did it work? Did it work? Were you successful?

3. How do you understand the meaning of evangelism? Do you practice it?

7

PRAYER: JUST PRAY MORE!

*"One day Jesus was praying in a certain place. When he finished,
one of his disciples said to him, "Lord, teach us to pray, just as
John taught his disciples." (Luke 11:1a)*

As a young pastor, when a parishioner came to me with a
problem, I would have the tendency to simply say, "Just
pray more!" That was not good advice. We all need to
learn **how** to pray and then we are off and running in our relationship
with God.

E. Stanley Jones had a lot to say about the importance of prayer.
He felt better or worse depending on how much time he set aside
each day to pray. Jones found that God faded out of his life to

the degree that prayer faded out. Jones affirmed that prayer is opening the channels from our emptiness to God's fullness, from our defeat to his victory!

So let's listen to Jones as he describes the process of learning to pray and listen to God.

- First, choose a favorable environment for your daily conversation with God,

- Then tell your heart that God is here with you.

- Still your mind and try not to rush to put things before God to grant! Let God put his finger on anything in your life that is not fully surrendered to his will. But if nothing comes up don't worry. God is not petty.

- Talk with God about what is on your mind so you can have a two way conversation. The most vital part may be not what you say to God, but what God will say to you, for God wants not merely to answer your prayer, he wants to make you into the kind of person through whom He can habitually answer prayer.

- Thank God for answering in his own way – it could be 'yes' or 'no.' No is an answer!

- If your mind happens to wonder, don't worry, simply take

the wandering thought and have it lead you back to God.

- Suppose an external interruption occurs, don't let that upset you.

- Suppose your prayer time is simply dull and dry. Don't let that upset you either. There are such dry and dull periods in every life. They need not disturb the fundamental joy of living. The glow in life will always return![1]

Jones spent at least two hours a day in prayer, and called his prayer time, his "listening post." He placed great emphasis on listening as an important element of his prayer life. It is no wonder that it was as if he were listening to the voice of God!

John Wesley was also an ardent believer in daily prayer. He began his prayer time at 5 a.m. I would like to suggest making prayer a priority in your life by setting aside time daily (1-2 hours throughout the day) to pray and listen for God's voice. You can pray when you wake, in your car, or as you go to sleep, and anytime throughout the day.

So, I no longer tell persons to "pray more." Rather than just praying "more", we can consider praying in a more meaningful way. We may start our prayer time by asking, "God, what do you wish to say to me today?"

We have much to learn from our brothers and sisters, the Quakers, for their practice of "meaningful silence." The more time we spend in prayer *meaningfully,* the more blessed we will be, and more able to bless others.

It may be helpful to write down your insights that come during your prayer time and keep a prayer journal. I've been asked many times, "Does prayer change things?" What I really know is that prayer changes people in a powerful way.

So, we do not have to understand the mystery of prayer, in order to pray more effectively. We must keep steadfast in our prayers, fully believing that miracles do happen. Sometimes, it helps to pray aloud, other times in silent contemplation. Sometimes, prayer changes things, but if not, prayer always changes us, simply by the act and discipline of praying daily.

And here is an important final point. In prayer, we do not bend God to our will, but we blend our will with God's. Prayer is primarily surrender and it is also assertion. After you have surrendered to the will of God, you can assert your will within that will. God then, according to E. Stanley Jones, can do things through us that he otherwise could not have done. Through prayer we begin to live by God's power. I know this sounds remarkable but it is true! Do try it!

Questions for Personal Reflection

We are submitting the following questions for personal reflection and small group discussions. Please use the rest of the pages for personal journaling or notes.

1. Prayer is an integral part of the Christian life. But the question is, "How do we pray in a meaningful and effective way?"

2. Do you have a disciplined prayer life? How does it work?

3. Can you share any practical results of your prayer life? How did it work for you?

8

ANXIETY: JUST DON'T WORRY!

"Do not be anxious about anything, but in every situation, by prayer and petition, with thanksgiving, present your requests to God." (Philippians 4:6)

I would venture to guess that most of us experience some anxiety and certainly all of us worry sometimes. Worry and anxiety seem to be a part of the human condition.

There are different kinds of anxiety. There is ontological anxiety, existential anxiety and just plain old worrying.

Ontological anxiety, according to the theologian Paul Tillich, is the kind of anxiety that we experience because of the fact of our humanness, our finite nature. Existential anxiety tends to arise during times of change, or when we are entering a new stage in life. Worrying is the kind of anxiety we may experience more often — worries are about specific things, sometimes trivial, on which, we sadly waste a lot of energy and time.

There is not much we can do about ontological anxiety, except to simply accept our finiteness, our limitations. With existential anxiety, we can admit that change can call into question meaning as we embark on a new path. We are sometimes fragile and sometimes we do have feet of clay.

Worrying is much more common and generally has a discrete focus. Managing our worries has to do with identifying the reason and cause of them. We could be worried about health, family, finances, job, or the future. Worry can be managed, if not eliminated, by discovering the source and finding ways to cope. Sometimes practical modifications help, such as wise planning, or practicing good time management skills. When you can focus on the present and not your past or future worries, you will find that the present moment is always the *divine* moment. Try it!

Jesus spoke a lot about the human inclination to worry and reassured us.

- Consider the lilies of the field. (Matthew 6:25)

- Seek first the kingdom of Heaven. (Matthew 6:33)

- Martha, Martha you are worrying about many things. (Luke 10:31)

- Do not worry about tomorrow. (Matthew 6:34)

And the Apostle Paul has much to teach us as well:

- Have no anxiety about anything. (Philippians 4-6)

Much of the worry we experience may be because we are always "in a hurry." The hardest thing for many of us is to be patient, and to learn how to slow down, and just be still. We are stressed or perhaps addicted to our personal technology, our computers, televisions, and social media. Being 'online' has become part of our daily ritual and existence. Many of us carry a Bluetooth device in our ear, so we can be instantly available by phone. Some of us leave our phones on at night, so we can receive texts, e-mails, and notifications throughout the evening hours when we should be getting needed sleep. Dare to be different—begining today set aside your devices for a couple of hours each day, and especially before you plan to go to sleep.

Re-read Chapter 7 on the importance of prayer. A prayer that can help alleviate **worry** is a prayer of contemplation, where you sit in total silence and truly listen for God. Don't ask God for anything, but rather allow the grace of God to invade and permeate your whole being. "Be still and know that I am God." (Psalm 46:10).

Questions for Personal Reflection

We are submitting the following questions for personal reflection and small group discussions. Please use the rest of the pages for personal journaling or notes.

1. Worry is a common experience in the life of every men and women everywhere. What worries you the most?

2. Worry is draining your energies. To what extent can you control or manage your worry or tendency to worry?

3. Anxiety is an integral part of the human condition. What examples in the Bible and passages can be helpful? Be specific.

Personal Notes

9

PAIN AND SUFFERING:
DON'T ASK WHY?

"I have told you these things, so that in me you may have peace. In this world you will have trouble. But take heart! I have overcome the world." (John 16:33)

D r. Scott M. Peck wrote the best-selling book, *The Road Less Travelled*. He begins the book with this rather intriguing comment.

Life is difficult. This is a great truth, one of the greatest truths. It is a great truth because once we truly see this truth, we transcend it. Once we truly know that life is difficult-once we truly understand and accept it-then life is no longer difficult. Because once it is accepted, the fact that life is difficult no longer matters.[1]

Interestingly enough, Jesus said this two thousand years ago. You *will* have tribulations, as noted in the above text from John.

Richard Rohr, a Franciscan Priest, wrote a book of daily meditations, with a rather captivating title: "Yes, And".[2] The thesis of Rohr's book is that the Gospel and the Christian faith is based on reality and thus is a realistic religion in our world. It is not an idealistic faith, but one that deals with the vicissitudes of life as it really is—life in the real world. "Jesus came to help us carry the legitimate pain of being human."[3] I know that our tendency is to deny or want to escape suffering, whatever it takes. However, sometimes suffering is the price we pay for living in a hurting and limited world. If anyone doubts that, just be reminded of the cross. That was reality!

Jones' book, *Christ and Human Suffering* shares his understanding of how Jesus addressed suffering.

Jesus accepted the face of human suffering. He does not explain it; much less does he explain it away. Had he undertaken to explain it, his gospel would have become a philosophy, in which case it would not have been a gospel. Jesus undertook to explain little, but changed everything in sight. His method of meeting pain and injustice was to transform them into something higher.[4]

Jones continues,

Don't bear trouble, use it...Take whatever happens, justice and injustice, pleasure and pain, compliments and criticism, take it up into the purpose of your life and make something of it. Turn it into a testimony.[5]

E. Stanley Jones had the occasion to make something of the debilitating brain stem stroke he suffered in 1971 and to use that event and affirm his YES to life. He surely did so!

I was with him at a Catholic retreat center in Oklahoma City when his stroke occurred on December 7. He was the evangelist, and I was teaching the Bible Hour for the Ashram. The stroke occurred during the night and Jones lay semiconscious on the floor, totally helpless. (There were no cell phones then, or lifeline buttons to summon assistance.)

The doors were locked, so no one could access his room. When he did not show up for the morning service, we were all very worried.

While I covered for his morning sessions, others managed to get into his room and he was rushed by ambulance to the local hospital.

Jones was subsequently transferred to rehabilitation hospitals in Boston where I visited him. It was close to Christmastime and someone brought a small artificial Christmas tree to his room. One day he gave it to Dorothy and me and we cherish it to this day. What a journey of fulfilling and rewarding ministry, pain, suffering and finally, victory. "I have told you this so that my joy may be in you and that your joy may be complete." (John 15:11)

Soon after his stroke, Brother Stanley began writing, or rather dictating, his final book, *The Divine Yes*, which I believe is one of his greatest books, in part because of the circumstances during which it was written.

While he was physically challenged, he was not mentally or emotionally impaired. He wrote the book in order to illustrate that the Christian faith provides us with the resources to have victory, in spite of even the most dire and adverse circumstances.

Jones took what happened to him and gave a victorious illustration about how he coped with that suffering. He writes:

I looked forward to a gentle descent into my nineties and perhaps beyond with nothing but gratitude for what God has wrought. Then suddenly, I found myself and my future apparently in ruins. My means of locomotion were shattered, and I could not recognize my voice on a tape recorder. The only hopeful thing was my intellect was not affected. Everything else had been changed.

But I said to myself, "Nothing has changed!" I'm still the same person that I was before the stroke. By prayer, I am still in communion with the same Person. Nothing had really changed except my means of communication with the outside world. The glorious thing was that my faith was not shattered. I was not holding it; it was holding me. Everything was intact. I can honestly say I wasn't asking, "My God, why?" I could and I can face the future with Him. Perhaps I can write this book by faith. If I can no longer preach a sermon, as I have trouble articulating words, why not **be** one?[6]

Like Job of the Old Testament, Brother Stanley undoubtedly wanted to understand why his stroke occurred. However, he quickly affirmed that his task, post stroke, was to glorify God, even during his current pain and suffering.

Jones, despite his stroke could say yes to life!

When we have no words that answer the 'why' of suffering, we can experience that we are not alone in our suffering. God is always present with us in our pain and suffering. We are never *alone*! Thanks be to God!

"For the Son of God, Jesus Christ, who was preached among you by us ... was not "Yes" and "No", but in him it has always been "Yes." He is the Yes pronounced upon God's promises, every one of them. (II Cor. 1:19-20)

What does it mean to say "Yes" to life in the midst of all circumstances? It means to confront reality with courage and be more than conquerors. *"No, in all these things we are more than conquerors through him who loved us."* (Romans 8:37)

To live in a state of "Yesness", means to say yes no matter what is happening to us." *I am not saying this because I am in need, for I have learned to be content..."* (Philippians 4:11-13).

When we can say 'Yes' to life, we can:

•   Cope with the present pandemic, with patience, courage, and perseverance, and not let it paralyze us or cause us to live in fear.

♦ Say yes to the future.

♦ Say yes to uncertainty.

♦ Say yes to failure and defeat knowing that because Christ arose, we will rise again.

♦ Say yes, and affirm that "because He lives, we can face tomorrow."′

To say yes to life means to face life unafraid! You, too, can say yes to life, because "YES" is another word for Jesus!

In the final analysis, there is no easy answer to the problem of pain and suffering, except to be "persons of grace" and to trust in the wisdom of the biblical text, which proclaims, "My grace is sufficient for you, for my power is made perfect in weakness... For when I am weak, then I am strong." (2 Corinthians 12:9-11)

Before we leave human suffering and the *Divine Yes,* I want to say a word about the suffering of brokenness? "He heals the brokenhearted and binds up their wounds." *(Psalm 147:3)*

I've experienced brokenness in my own life and as a consequence, I've developed a great sensitivity and empathy for the suffering and pain of others. Henri Nouwen's writing about the 'wounded healer' has deeply influenced my own ministry. He writes,

"Who can listen to a story of loneliness and despair without taking the risk of experiencing similar pains in his own heart and even losing his precious peace of mind?" In short, "Who can take away suffering without entering it?"[8]

I do my best to share in the suffering of others with empathy and love. The reflections of the Chilean poet, Amado Nervo are very meaningful to me.

"Muy cerca del ocaso, yo te bendigo vida.
Vida, nada me debes. Vida, estamos en paz."

(Translation: As I come to the close of my life's journey, I bestow my blessings upon Life. Life, you do not owe me anything. Life, we are at peace with each other.)

At this point in my journey, I humbly give thanks for my life. I concur with Nervo, "Life, you do not owe me anything. Life, we are at peace with each other." It is so reassuring!

Questions for Personal Reflection

We are submitting the following questions for personal reflection and small group discussions. Please use the rest of the pages for personal journaling or notes.

1. How many times have you wondered about the mystery of pain and suffering? There are no real answers, but if you could, would you have any suggestions?

2. Do you spend a lot of time worrying? Why? Could you begin to ask, "How can I stop this habit"?

3. How can you help someone else who is experiencing hopelessness, pain and suffering? Do you think that it is physical or emotional?

Read II Corinthians 12:9 together. What does it mean to you?

4. Do you believe in miracles? They happen all the time! You may even be one — a miracle of grace.

10

HEALING AND WHOLENESS:
THE WILL TO LIVE

"The Spirit of the Lord is on me, because he has anointed me to proclaim good news to the poor. He has sent me to proclaim freedom for the prisoners and recovery of sight for the blind, to set the oppressed free, to proclaim the year of the Lord's favor..."
(Luke 4:18-20)

One of the most significant aspects of the Christian Ashram program is the Healing and Wholeness Service, which is offered during every Ashram.

The significant part of this service is that it includes not only healing, but *wholeness*. I have been persuaded that it was genius on the part of E. Stanley Jones to emphasize body, mind and spirit in his books and sermons. Therefore, *wholeness* should always be part of the healing.

During my life, I have been greatly inspired by the lyrics of the hymn, *"Heal me, Hands of Jesus."* A portion of it reads, "Cleanse me, blood of Jesus, take bitterness away; let me forgive as one forgiven and bring me peace today."[1]

I believe that wholeness includes experiencing forgiveness, releasing bitterness, including memories of guilt and regrets, and, that experience brings peace within, which so aptly the hymn conveys. "Fill me, joy of Jesus; anxiety shall cease, and heaven's serenity be mine, for Jesus brings me peace!"[2]

The Ashram offers an experience of Jesus Christ and through that experience enables fractured and partial persons to become whole persons. Many of us attend an Ashram every year to be transformed again and again in some new aspect of our lives.

Persons outside of the Ashram family are not aware of what we have to offer through the Ashram experience. It offers "not only healing, but wholeness."

I remain convinced that the Ashram is the *best-kept secret.* I want to continue to share the good news of this vital ministry, a profound ministry that offers personal, emotional, and spiritual healing and wholeness through the hands of Jesus offered in the Christian Ashram experience.

Questions for Personal Reflection

We are submitting the following questions for personal reflection and small group discussions. Please use the rest of the pages for personal journaling or notes.

1. Have you ever experienced healing? How does it work?

2. Which of the healing miracles in the Bible are most meaningful to you? Explain why.

3. How do you help persons who need healing and wholeness?

4. How does one cope with the awful consequences of the pandemic?

5. What negative emotions, such as resentment, fear, worry and anxiety, self-condemnation, and the like, continue to torment your life? Are you willing to surrender them?

6. What about your personal quiet time? Do you feel disciplined enough to observe it religiously? Are you discouraged or depressed? What do you plan to do about it?

11

LOVE: MORE POWERFUL
THAN THE ATOM

"And now these three remain: faith, hope and love. But the greatest of these is love." (I Cor. 13:13)

No collection of my observations would be complete with out including mention of perhaps the most important word in the human vocabulary—love. It is so important, that in Greek there are several words that attribute specific meanings to love. There is "Eros," which is romantic love; "Philia," which is brotherly love, and then, "Agape", which is divine or unconditional love.

We have all experienced these three expressions of love.

There is power in love. It can melt someone's heart to hear the words, "I love you." It may be said from one lover to another, or to a father, mother, son, or daughter. Regardless of the recipient, it can make the person feel that his or her life really matters! Love is the highest in God and the deepest in us, and thus, according to E. Stanley Jones, love is the most beautiful thing on our planet.[1]

Frederick Buechner brings another important perspective when he writes, "Of all powers, love is the most powerful and the most powerless. It is the most powerful because it alone can conquer that final and most impregnable stronghold that is the human heart. It is the most powerless because it can do nothing except by consent."

I have often asked if love is a matter of the will or is it an emotion? Frederick Buechner writes:

In the Christian sense, love is not primarily an emotion, but an act of the will. When Jesus tells us to love our neighbors, he is not telling us to love them in the sense of responding to them with a cozy emotional feeling. On the contrary, he is telling us to love our neighbors in the sense of being willing to work for their well-being even if it means sacrificing our own well-being to that end, even if it means sometimes just leaving them alone. Thus in Jesus' terms, we can love our neighbors without necessarily liking them.

In fact liking them may stand in the way of loving them by making us overprotective sentimentalists instead of reasonably honest friends.[2]

Jones helps us close out this chapter,

From every side, life is converging on one point, love. That desire for somebody to love us and to love somebody is the deepest thing in life and the highest in God. So the deepest in us and the highest in God do not conflict, they coincide and we are the beneficiaries.[3]

Questions for Personal Reflection

We are submitting the following questions for personal reflection and small group discussions. Please use the rest of the pages for personal journaling or notes.

1. What is your favorite definition of love? How do you practice loving someone? Do you feel loved now?

2. Love is an integral part of reality. What are some tangible ways in which you are sure love is real or becomes a reality?

3. When you say, "God loves you," what kind of response do you receive? Meditate on the needs and expectations of the other person. What messages are you sending? How are you sensitive to that other person?

12

WHAT IS AN ASHRAM:
THE BEST-KEPT SECRET?

"They devoted themselves to the apostles' teaching and to fellowship, to the breaking of bread and to prayer." (Acts 2:42)

In 1930, E. Stanley Jones with the assistance of Indian Christian minister, Rev. Yunas Sinha and Ethel Turner, a recently retired English missionary, bought 350 acres in the foothills of the Himalayas, establishing the Sat Tal Christian Ashram. Jones sought an intentional Christian community, one whose group discipline would benefit him as well as other Ashram participants. Jones also believed that the Christian faith, as a universal faith, would benefit from translation into indigenous forms to express its message. He used the term Ashram to express this group fellowship and

Christianized the Ashram experience by making adaptations to the Indian Ashram that would reflect the Christian message. This very successful and meaningful Christian retreat, which Jones affirmed was one of the most significant contributions of his ministry, was transplanted to America in 1940.

The early Ashrams in North America lasted about one week. Now, most Ashrams last from three to four days, as few of us have lots of available vacation time. To increase the availability of Ashrams, we have instituted mini-Ashrams, held in nursing homes, retirement centers, on college campuses and in local churches, so that more people experience what an Ashram can contribute to spiritual health. I've always felt that the Ashram is much more than an organization. The Ashram is really a movement inspired by the Holy Spirit.

There are Christian Ashrams across North America and many around the world. Each year more than 1,500 people experience the depth and transforming power of a Christian Ashram. We hope to keep increasing the number of people who attend Ashrams and share this unique experience more broadly in North America and throughout the world.

The Ashram is governed by a national Board of Directors, which are elected every three years. There is an Executive Director, who oversees the administration and related business matters for the Ashram. The office manager cares for administrative duties, including accounting, correspondence, e-mail, and telephone calls.

Jones was often asked this question: "What does it take to become a member of the Ashram Group?" His answer was: "We have one qualification and only one. 'Do you want to be different? If you want to be different come on, but if you don't want to be different, can do nothing for you.' The crux of being made different is found in self surrender. Only when the self is *surrendered* can you cultivate your spiritual life around the new center – Christ. Then everything falls into its place."[1]

As this quotation states, the key word in the Ashram is "surrender", meaning release or letting go. E. Stanley Jones meant for it to be an intentional decision to let go of one's past, including guilts, anxiety about the future, self-condemnation, fear, and other troubling emotions. He stressed particularly the surrender of "the self", so that we are no longer self-centered persons, but rather Christ-centered persons.

If we were to share the secret to the Ashram's success, I would say that the Ashram is an occasion to experience the redemptive power of the love of our Lord, Jesus Christ.

Another way to describe the Ashram is to say, it is an experience of "the Kingdom of God" in miniature. If we can move to discover what the Kingdom of God would be, then we would agree that it includes several significant elements. The Ashram contains each of these important elements and offers:

- A place of total acceptance, regardless of circumstances.
- A place where unconditional love is practiced.
- A place where a person can be totally honest about his/her weaknesses and shortcomings, without fear of rejection.
- A place where communication with God is encouraged and supported daily.
- A place where personal and private counseling can take place.
- A place where creative silence and reflection can become a meaningful spiritual discipline.
- A place of serious, personal spiritual reflection and growth.

The word Ashram has perhaps been perplexing. Some persons may find the word mysterious or perhaps related to a mystical experience of eastern religions. It is a Sanskrit word meaning, "away from hard labor," a place and time of rest, relaxation, apart from the stress and pressures of the world.

While the Ashram can be described in many ways, it really needs to be experienced in its fullness for participants to come to know the deep meaning the Ashram experience holds for their lives.

The first meeting at the Ashram is the Open Heart, which is a corporate catharsis. The participants are given an opportunity to answer the questions, "Why have you come? What do you want? What do you really need?" It is a way of allowing persons to engage in a process of public and supportive self-examination. Persons willingly share their deepest needs, which is cathartic.

During the Morning Watch, a devotional period, we are all asked to read a particular passage from the New Testament as we sit in silence for 30 minutes reflecting on the scriptural reading. For the next half hour, we are invited to share our insights with the group about what we have read. All participants become teachers and all participants become students who are taught.

A Bible Hour, for the Bible reveals Jesus, follows breakfast and is designed to target the needs shared in the Morning of the Open Heart by drawing on specific Biblical verses. By scripture-based teaching, participants can learn how to interpret and reflect on God's word as written in the Bible.

The Work Hour is an opportunity to be of service and work with our hands. This time together gives us both recreation and re-creation when our bodies are attached to constructive purposes such as tidying up the physical environment of the Ashram.

The afternoon is devoted for personal counseling, rest and recreation and Prayer Groups. The Prayer Group is not for the discussion of prayer, but an occasion to enter into intensive intercessory prayer for the needs of others, specific persons, or for global matters and concerns.

A Prayer Vigil goes on 24 hours each day and Ashram members sign up for selected hours. Prayer requests are entered into a Prayer Vigil Book, which is accessible to Ashram participants, enabling them to pray for the specific needs of others.

Every Ashram selects one evening to celebrate communion, often as a part of the Healing and Wholeness Service. We explain that we are not 'healers,' but are lending our hands to Christ, for his healing to come through us. This is a very symbolic and meaningful experience. The Christian Ashram does not make physical heath the emphasis. Rather, self-surrender and conversion are emphasized, which often results in remediation and freedom from physical disease.

The evening Evangelism Hour is the occasion for the lead evangelist to teach/preach on a variety of subjects, such as the

Holy Spirit, the Kingdom of God, conversion, and the power of surrender.

Silent Hours are observed every night beginning at 11:00 p.m. until the Morning Watch, when the leader breaks the silence by affirming, "The Lord is risen." And the people respond, "The Lord is risen indeed. Jesus is Lord!"

The final element of the Ashram program is the hour of the Overflowing Heart, where participants discover the Ashram fellowship has become redemptive. Problems and anxieties of participants are "dissolved" in the context of the redemptive group experience.[2]

Ninety-five percent of persons who attend an Ashram will experience a deep transformation.

On the final day, there is the farewell and goodbye blessing, as we sing, "Blest be the tie that binds", and in unison affirm "unreservedly given to God, unbreakably given to one other."[3]

As noted earlier, the focus of the Ashram is to be the kingdom of God in miniature. This means we create a climate of loving and caring acceptance, where every person feels that he/she "belongs" and is accepted, regardless of ethnicity, disability, reputation, occupation, or economic status.

God is in the business of changing our lives and making new creations, every day, if we will allow Him to work in our lives. (See, II

Corinthians 5:17-18). The Christian Ashram is in the transformation business. We must continue to keep that intention at the forefront, particularly in the midst of a post-pandemic, post-modern world and our rapidly changing and evolving cultural milieu.

I'm convinced that the Ashram is one of the best-kept secrets in the church world. People in our local churches are missing the opportunity to experience this significant way of enriching Christian life! We can and must do better in spreading excitement about this unique experience in the years ahead. The Ashram movement has continued to thrive through eighty years of redemptive ministry and we hope to continue for the next eighty years and beyond.

May the Ashram continue to thrive forever. Jesus is Lord!

Questions for Personal Reflection

We are submitting the following questions for personal reflection and small group discussions. Please use the rest of the pages for personal journaling or notes.

1. Have you ever attended a Christian Ashram? What was the most meaningful part of it?

2. Do you know someone who could benefit by attending an ashram? Could you tell them about it?

3. Do you wish Jesus to abide in your heart? If so, just open your heart to experience Him.

4. Self-centeredness brings misery in every situation. Are you familiar with the term "abuse of kindness"? What does it mean to you?

CONCLUSION

"Therefore, if anyone is in Christ, the new creation has come; The old has gone, the new is here!" (II Cor. 5:17-18)

All of E. Stanley Jones' books are "outstanding." However, if I were to choose one, I would select, *How to Be A Transformed Person*. Why? Because it addresses the fundamental invitation to be a changed person. The more I think about the genius of the Ashram, I have concluded that it is designed to have people become transformed persons. Many of us wish to be made different, to be transformed, but 'how'? The experience at a Christian Ashram will tell you all you need to know about that 'how.' Please do join us! Jesus is Lord!

Personal Notes

AFTERWORD

There are some wonderful books about faith in which the author presents the results of excellent research and provides important information. They inform the reader, promote new understandings, and generate imaginative responses.

There are also wonderful books about faith in which the author offers inspiration and guidance in the disciplines of discipleship. They serve as resources for leadership and witness in the life of the church.

And there are also wonderful books about faith in which the author invites the reader into a personal journey of remembrance, insight, and hope. The new little book by Roberto Escamilla is such a volume. Titled *Beacons of Hope*, it is a gem. Everyone who reads it will be grateful for the wisdom of the E. Stanley Jones Foundation in choosing to publish it.

Dr. Escamilla warmly recalls in each chapter an aspect or event in his own life when he was touched by E. Stanley Jones. From important events in the Ashram movement to poignant personal episodes in the life of the late Dr. Jones, the reader will discover or rediscover some of the greatness that was manifest in the ministry of the most eminent twentieth century mission evangelist.

Moreover, Dr. Escamilla also offers the benefits of his own

experiences and insights. His list of things to consider about preaching in chapter four is simply superb. His practical advice on the topic of conversion in chapter six is remarkably fresh and useful.

In the Introduction, Dr. Escamilla calls this his "final book." It may be. But he has much to say, and he does so in a loving way in these pages. Whether there are any more pages that ever come from his pen, these in *Beacons of Hope* are to be treasured.

William B. Lawrence

Dean, SMU's Perkins School of Theology and Professor of American Church History, 2002-2016

NOTES

Introduction

1 Paul Tillich, *The Shaking of the Foundations* (New York, Scribner's, 1948), See, https://quotefancy.com/paul-tillich-quotes

Chapter 2

1 Eunice Jones Mathews and James K. Mathews, *Selections from E. Stanley Jones: Christ and Human Need* (Potomac, MD: The E. Stanley Jones Foundation, 2021), 32.

2 Bill and Gloria Gaither, "There's Just Something About That Name," (1970). *United Methodist Hymnal,* 171.

Chapter 3

1 E. Stanley Jones, *The Christ of the Mount* (The E. Stanley Jones Foundation, (ESJF 2017), 34.

2 E. Stanley Jones, *Christ at the Round Table* (ESJF, 2019), 261.

3 E. Stanley Jones, *The Christ of the Mount* (ESJF, 2017), 206.

Chapter 4

1 Kate Hankey, "I Love to Tell the Story" (1866), *United Methodist Hymnal,* 156.

2 Fred B. Craddock, *Preaching* (Nashville, TN: Abingdon Press, 1985).

Chapter 5

1 Charles Albert Tindley "The Storms of Life are Raging" (1905). *United Methodist Hymnal,* 512.

2 E. Stanley Jones, *Christ and Human Suffering* (ESJF, 2021), 85.

Chapter 6

1 E. Stanley Jones, *Conversion,* (ESJF, 2019), 39.

Chapter 7

1 E. Stanley Jones, *How to Pray* (Nashville, TN: Upper Room Books, 2015), 21-27.

Chapter 9

1 Scott M. Peck, *The Road Less Traveled* (New York: Touchstone Publishers, 1978), 15.

2 Richard Rohr, *Yes, And* (Cincinnati, Ohio, Franciscan Media, 2013).

3 E. Stanley Jones, *A Song of Ascents* (Nashville, TN: Abingdon, 1968), 149.

4 E. Stanley Jones, *Christ and Human Suffering* (ESJF, 2021), 72.

5 E. Stanley Jones, *Christ and Human Suffering* (ESJF, 2021), 73.

6 E. Stanley Jones, *The Divine Yes* (Nashville, TN: Abingdon Press, 1975), 30-31.

7 Bill and Gloria Gaither "Because He Lives"(1970). *United Methodist Hymnal*, 364.

8 Henri J. M. Nouwen, *The Wounded Healer: Ministry in Contemporary Society* (Cokesbury,1979). See, https://quotes.pub/q/who-can-listen-to-a-story-of-loneliness-and-despair-without—192150

Chapter 10

1 Michael A. Perry "Heal me Hands of Jesus"(1982), (2nd verse). *United Methodist Hymnal*, 262.

2 Michael A. Perry "Heal me Hands of Jesus"(1982), (4th verse). *United Methodist Hymnal*, 262.

Chapter 11

1 E. Stanley Jones, *Conversion* (ESJF 2019), 93.

2 On Buechner, see, https://www.frederickbuechner.com/quote-of-the-day/2016/6/29/love (accessed 9/18/2021)

3 E. Stanley Jones, *Conversion* (ESJF 2019), 93.

Chapter 12

1 E. Stanley Jones, *A Song of Ascents* (Cokesbury, 1968), 231.

2 For a complete history of the Christian ashram, please refer to *A History of the Christian Ashram in North America* by Anne Mathews-Younes.

3 E. Stanley Jones, *A Song of Ascents,* 225.

ABOUT
THE AUTHOR

DR. ROBERTO ESCAMILLA was born in Mexico in 1931. He earned the S.T.M. from Perkins School of Theology in 1955. He has served as a United Methodist pastor in Dallas, San Antonio, and Austin, Texas. He also served as President for the Board of Directors of the United Christian Ashram International. He has served on the Board of the Board of Global Ministries, with the Board of Discipleship, as Associate General Secretary and as Editor of The Upper Room (Spanish edition). Escamilla earned a B.S. from Parsons College and a B.A. from Iowa Wesleyan College; an M.A. from Trinity University in San Antonio; an S.T.M. from Union Theological Seminary; and a D.Min. from Vanderbilt University.

Roberto has been married for more than 65 years to the former Dorothy Mae Delaplain. They have four adult children, ten grandchildren and one great-grandchild. They currently reside in Pittstown, Oklahoma.

ABOUT
E. STANLEY JONES

REV. DR. E. STANLEY JONES (1884-1973) was described by a distinguished Bishop as the "greatest missionary since Saint Paul.[1] This missionary/evangelist spent seventy years in the ministry of the Methodist Church and of Jesus Christ. He was an Evangelist, apostle, missionary, author of twenty-seven books, statesman, Bishop-elect (who resigned before ordination), founder of Christian Ashrams, ecumenical leader, and spokesman for peace, racial brotherhood, and social justice, and constant witness for Jesus Christ. Jones was a confidant of President Franklin D. Roosevelt. He was nominated twice for the Nobel Peace Prize, and his ministry in India brought him into close contact with that country's leaders including Jawaharlal Nehru, Rabindranath Tagore, and Mahatma Gandhi. He foresaw where the great issues would be and spoke to them long before they were recognized, often at great unpopularity and even antagonism and derision to himself. Many considered Jones a prophet and his honors and he did receive them, were all laid at the feet of Jesus Christ.

Jones wrote 27 books. More than 3.6 million copies of his books have been sold and they have been translated into 30 languages.

Jones wrote and spoke for the general public and there is little doubt that his words brought hope and refreshment to multitudes all over the world. As a well-known, engaging, and powerful evangelist, Jones delivered tens of thousands of sermons and lectures. He typically traveled fifty weeks a year, often speaking two to six times a day.

Jones worked to revolutionize the whole theory and practice of missions to third world nations by disentangling Christianity from Western political and cultural imperialism. He established hundreds of Christian Ashrams throughout the world, many of which still meet today.

Even after a severe stroke at the age of 87 robbed him of his speech, Jones managed to dictate into a tape recorder his last book, *The Divine Yes*. He died in India on January 25, 1973. Jones monumental accomplishments in life emerged from the quality of his character cultivated through his intimacy with Jesus Christ. As he lived in Christ, he reflected Christ. That experience is available to us when we invite Christ to live in us!

Note

1 Bishop James K. Mathews (1913-2010).

CONTACT DETAILS

For further information about the Christian Ashram,
please contact:

Lisa Chandler
Email: uca@christianashram.org

Mailing Address for UCA:

United Christian Ashram International
904 Deville Lane
Ruston, LA 71270
Telephone: (318) 232-0004
Website: www.christianashramint.org

For further information about the E. Stanley Jones Foundation,
please contact:

Anne Mathews-Younes
Email: anne@estanleyjonesfoundation.com

Mailing Address for the E. Stanley Jones Foundation (ESJF):

The E. Stanley Jones Foundation
10804 Fox Hunt Lane
Potomac, MD 20854
Telephone: (240) 328-5115
Website: www.estanleyjonesfoundation.com

Made in the USA
Coppell, TX
21 April 2022